LIFE calling

a 5-session course //
on vocation //
for Lent //

CHURCH HOUSE
PUBLISHING

Church House Publishing
Church House
Great Smith Street
London SW1P 3NZ

Tel: 020 7898 1451
Fax: 020 7898 1449

ISBN 978-0-7151-4137-3

Published 2007 by
Church House Publishing

Cover design by S2 design and advertising
Printed by Creative Print and Design Group
Ebbw Vale, Wales

Contents

Acknowledgements

The authors and publishers would like to thank the following groups and individuals for their invaluable help in trialling and offering feedback on this course:

Peter Ball; Canon Katrina Barnes and groups at St Augustine's Bromley Common; Joanna Cox; Revd Mike Hall and Cannon Lane Methodist Church House Group; Sheridan James's cell group, West Streatham; Anna Potts and a group at Enfield Baptist Church; Cathie Rutter and the Monday Evening Fellowship Group, Holy Trinity Ripon.

The authors and publisher gratefully acknowledge permission to reproduce copyright material in this book. Every effort has been made to trace and contact copyright holders. If there are any inadvertent omissions we apologize to those concerned and will ensure that a suitable acknowledgement is made in all future editions.

The Methodist Covenant Prayer on pages 64–65 from the *Methodist Worship Book* is copyright © Trustees for Methodist Church Purposes 1999.

The prayer on page 44 from Janet Morley, *All Desires Known*, SPCK, 1992, is copyright © Janet Morley and is reproduced by permission of SPCK.

The Mrs Fidget story in Appendix 2 from *The Four Loves* by C.S. Lewis is copyright © C.S. Lewis Pte Ltd, 1960 and used by permission.

Extracts from *God of Surprises* by Gerard Hughes, copyright © 1985, *Live for a Change* by Francis Dewar, copyright © 1988 and *The Divine Embrace* by Christina Rees, copyright © 2006, used by permission of Darton, Longman & Todd Ltd.

>> Introduction

Life Calling is an exploration of what vocation is about: the call to know God and to allow that relationship to direct, shape and transform all of life. The focus is not just on what we do in the church, or in our working life, but on the deeper issues of how we see and handle the whole of life.

>>Why explore vocation?

'Vocation' is a word that has been shrinking for decades. Originally it expressed the birthright of every baptized person – a call to know God and live in the light of that relationship. It then became focused on what today we would define as our work, career or profession. It was then further restricted to 'the caring professions' – clergy, teachers, doctors and nurses. More recently, the word has come to be used exclusively to refer to ordained ministry.

As a result, many people have lost all sense of their life calling – that which God has made them to be and do. The truth is that God has made each of us in his own image, and calls us to follow him, discovering and exercising the particular skills and gifts he has given us, growing into the unique fullness of the person he has called us to be and sharing in his work of bringing all creation to its intended wholeness.

Few of us would set out for a day's walking in the mountains without a route plan and map. But many of us embark on the different stages of our lives with little thought about our direction and purpose. From time to time it is helpful to stop and take stock of this, to reconsider our priorities and to reorient ourselves around the God who:

> calls us by name and knows us (Isaiah 43.1;
>   1 Corinthians 13.12);
> creates us as 'living images' of himself (Genesis 1.27);
> gives each of us particular skills and abilities
>   (Exodus 35.30-35; 1 Corinthians 12.27-28);

> helps us to leave behind the things that distract us and separate us from him (Romans 6.12-14);

> sends us out to live lives that reflect the love of God to others (Matthew 5.14-16).

Life Calling is designed to help in this process of reflection and exploration.

Each one is created differently with an individual call which no other human being can answer for us.
Gerard Hughes in Francis Dewar, Live for a Change, *p. ix*

Our vocation is not alien to our creation:
it is the fulfilment of what we have been created for.
David Ford, The Shape of Living, *p. 35*

>>What does the course consist of?

There are five sessions each designed to last 90 minutes. Each session covers one major aspect of our being called by God. The course explores the principles undergirding vocation, as well as helping all participants grow in their awareness of God's call in their lives. It does so while recognizing the unique way that God calls each of us: Our vocation is as individual as our fingerprints.

> **Session 1: Called by God**
Looks at the shape of God's call as seen in Scripture and explores how that works out in our lives. Vocation begins with God.

> **Session 2: Called from within**
Although the call comes from God, it is the drawing out of what he has planted in us, not the imposing of something foreign to our nature. It is the expression of his image in which we have been made. However, we usually have to dig to find it.

> **Session 3: Called out**
The good news is that God's call sets us free from pressures we put upon ourselves, and others place upon us. Yet there is a cost, for God calls us out of our narrow pursuits, our comfort zones and our addictions. His call sets us free to share in his purposes of love.

> **Session 4: Called up**
> God calls us to join in with his loving care of the world, part of
> which involves enlisting us in the work of bringing it to
> wholeness. For some that means a lifelong 'vocation'; but for
> most of us it is about a life-giving way of living an 'ordinary'
> life. It is about being in step with the heartbeat of the universe.

> **Session 5: Called on**
> To live life in response to God's call is to embark on an adventure,
> a journey through life in which we make a contribution to the
> world around us. This session explores how we can grow in our
> sense of calling beyond the end of the course.

The theme of each session is developed by means of engagement with
some teaching input, a passage of Scripture, reflecting on our life, praying
together and interactive ideas designed to engage with our imaginative
capacities, not just our ability to think and reason. Each session ends with
ideas for living out the truths that have been explored.

>>How each session works

Material for the course is in two sections for each session – *Beforehand*
and *The Session*. *Beforehand* is designed to help leaders prepare to take
a group through *The Session*.

For more detailed briefing notes on each session, see p. 8.

Making the most of the course

Life Calling is designed to be complete in itself. However, the value of the
course can be increased significantly by approaching it as a Lenten
discipline, giving time, thought and effort to living out what we have
grasped in the sessions. To this end participants are encouraged to:

> **Keep a journal:** We encourage all participants to buy a journal
> (or they could be given one at the first session). You don't have
> to be a good writer to keep a journal. No one else is going to
> read it – let alone mark it! Use it for notes, sketches, questions
> to record your thoughts, feelings, insights and experiences
> about your sense of 'calling' as well as for working with the
> exercises suggested in the sessions. Equally you can use it to

paste in comments or pictures you find in newspapers and magazines that speak to you about some aspect of vocation. Keeping a journal is a great way to have a conversation with oneself, the material and God. It disciplines us to stop in order to reflect on where we are going and what really matters. Alternatively, or in addition, to keeping a journal . . .

> **Talk it over with a friend/prayer partner.** For some, this may be an easier way of exploring the material further; for others, this would work well as a supplement to keeping a journal. This can be done either with another member of the group or with someone who is not part of it.

> **Practise:** doing one or more of the *Practise!* suggestions at the end of each session, not least the spiritual disciplines outlined there. They can help us develop a sense of vocation in the whole of our living.

Life Calling as a whole-church process

Church leaders can support the course in several ways. Why not use the course as an opportunity to consider calling and vocation as a whole church?

Church leaders might want to consider:

> **Sermon series:** running a parallel sermon series looking at biblical accounts of personal call.

> **Pastoral care:** Helping people (through one-to-one work) to discover their personal call.

> **Testimony/prayer:** most church members' primary area of calling is beyond the organizational life of the church. Ask a vet, shopkeeper, tax officer, or designer (to name a few examples of the range of occupations) in the congregation to share their experience of their work and faith in a Sunday service and then have them lead the intercessions. (Don't forget to include those whose current chapter of life involves retirement, being a full-time parent or carer, unemployment, etc.)

> **Commissioning:** Ordinations are major events for clergy, but what do we do for those called to run a charity shop, or lead children's work, or co-ordinate the local Council's response to global warming, or teach immigrants English? Commissioning affirms vocation and service.

> **Vocations Sunday** always takes place on the fourth Sunday of Easter. If you are running *Life Calling* during Lent, why not plan to have a post-Easter celebration on this date? There are worship and other resources on the web link **www.chpublishing.co.uk/lifecalling** and more on the Vocations Sunday site, see **www.cofe-ministry.org.uk/vocsun**.

>>Tips for leaders: Managing the group

Group size

An ideal size for a group would be 8 to 12 people. All groups can benefit from dividing into small groups (twos and threes) for the discussion times so that everyone has the opportunity to contribute.

To get the most out of the course, we suggest that each group member has a copy of the book.

Who can lead the course?

Most people, with preparation, could lead this course. The leader's main task is to enable discussion and exploration to take place, rather than to lecture the group. The task is simply to take people through the material as it is set out. It is also good to delegate parts of the session (see below under *Delegate*).

Where should we meet?

Wherever you meet, make sure the room is comfortable, warm and easy for everyone to get to see everyone else. If splitting into pairs or triplets, remember that two groups in a room tend to distract each other but three or more such groups are fine as you cannot hear what is going on in the other groups. However, be aware that the hard of hearing may struggle with background noise.

You may like to provide refreshments before or after the sessions. Be aware, if you do so, that extra time needs to be added to the 90 minutes of the session.

To help lead the group we offer some tips below. The booklet *Leading an Emmaus Group* (see Bibliography) is a real help with this task.

>>Running a session

Be prepared

Make sure you are familiar with the material. Read through both the *Beforehand* section and *The Session* itself. Decide which parts you will use, given the amount of time available and the nature of your group. If you want to use any of the multimedia or more interactive suggestions, you will need to source the materials: a list is given at the start of the *Beforehand* section. You will also need to decide whether to work in smaller groups for some of the activities, and if you need to ask others to help with some parts of the session.

Leaders are encouraged to read through the *Detailed briefing notes* (pp. 8 ff) at the start of their preparation for each session.

Using the Input background material

It is best not to read out from any source in the session, but to put background ideas and information into your own words. Remember: the aim of the sessions is to help people explore the subject, not tell them what to think or do. The leader's task is to help people discover a greater sense of call from God in their lives by working together on the material provided.

The Input part of the *Encounter* section needs preparation beforehand. Keep it brief, making a few points clearly. The more you practise what you are going to say, the less you will need to simply read out notes.

Delegate

Don't do everything yourself: share out tasks with others. Not only does this help you, it gives others the chance to develop and explore their gifts and talents as leaders. Invite others to read the Bible passage, do the refreshments or welcome people. Leadership of *Encounter* and *Do something* sections, as well as the prayer elements and the various discussion points, can be delegated. Good leading draws out the gifts of all rather than depending on the gifts of one person.

Give people plenty of warning. Don't land them with difficult jobs at the last minute. Be available to give support and advice if needed. Give 'leaders' the chance to look at the material beforehand.

Be organized

> Get to the venue in good time so that you are not doing last-minute preparations as people are arriving.

> Set the room up carefully so there is room for everyone and they can all see each other, the leader, TV and DVD player, etc.

> Make sure you have all the pens, paper, craft materials, music, etc. needed. Note the checklist at the start of each *Beforehand* section.

Be imaginative

People learn in different ways: some take in information by reading and quiet reflection, others through discussion, others respond best to visual stimuli (so value a visual focus for worship). Others respond best through music, craft, or doing things. The course provides you with a range of resources to work in these varied ways. We encourage you not to do what is easiest for you but what is most likely to engage and challenge the group. Be inventive and use your own and the group's creativity. Draw on the skills of any in the group who have gifts and experience in these other ways of learning.

Be flexible

There is enough material for a ninety-minute session; **but suggested timings are intended as rough guides not tight rules.** Be free to move quickly through some sections or miss them out altogether. It's better to do a few activities thoroughly than rush everything and leave people feeling exhausted.

>>Detailed briefing notes

Material for each session is in two sections – *Beforehand* and *The Session*.

Beforehand contains information to help leaders prepare the session:
> **Aim** of the session.
> **What you will need** – a checklist of practical materials and things to think through before the session.
> **Background** to the theme of the session and notes on the Bible passage. Ideally, this material should be summarized by the leader during the Input part of the session rather than read out verbatim.

The Session is structured under the following headings:

 Welcome

 Pray

 Action replay (except in session 1)

 Time to share

 Encounter

 Do something

 Apply within

 Pray

 Practise!

The sections of the course work in the following way:

>>Welcome (5 minutes)

The first task of the leader is to welcome people and put them at their ease. If the group is meeting for the first time then make time in the first session for people to introduce themselves. You might like to do that by asking people to: 'tell us your name and something you particularly enjoy doing' or divide into pairs, give the pairs five minutes to introduce themselves to each other, then ask individuals to ask their partner to introduce them to the rest of the group.

>>Pray (5–10 minutes)

This opening prayer time is designed to help people become still after what, for many, is likely to have been a busy day. It offers an opportunity to 'draw breath before God'.

This, and the closing meditation, is a very suitable part to delegate to someone else; for it to be done creatively will take preparation time and imaginative thought.

In handling the prayer times it helps to create a still atmosphere, light a candle, play some music or provide a visual focus such as a cross or image of Christ, an icon, group of stones and driftwood, or a still picture or DVD (e.g. waterfall, tree, planets).

Whoever leads the prayer elements needs to decide how the actual praying is to be handled. It can be done:
> in silence;
> by using biddings;
> by extemporary prayer.

Different approaches suit different types of prayer. Also, some groups will be more or less familiar with extemporary prayer. Make sure, before the praying begins, that people know how it is being handled.

>>Action replay (5 minutes)

An opportunity for group members to report back on the practice they agreed to undertake from the previous week's *Practise!* section.

>>Time to share (5 minutes)

Two quotations and questions are provided as a way in to the week's theme. The questions can be discussed as a whole group or in pairs.

>>Encounter (20–25 minutes)

There are three parts to this section:

> **a. Input**
> Based on his or her reading of the *Input* notes, the leader introduces the subject for the session (some group members may prefer to read these notes themselves).

> **b. Read the Bible passage**
> Ask a volunteer – but do so well before the meeting.

> **c. Talk about it**
> Questions are supplied to help the group explore the passage. You can use your own questions here. Split into twos or threes if it is a large group.

>>Do something (20 minutes)

Many of us grasp things best by intuition, by seeing and by doing, working more with our imagination than with logic. This is the approach taken in this section, which offers a film clip to watch and discuss and one other interactive activity – choose one. This is another appropriate part of the course to ask someone to take on – though ask them well in advance.

A note on Billy Elliot

In several of the sessions we have suggested the option of using clips from the film *Billy Elliot*. It is the story of a young boy who discovers an innate gift for dance, which is fostered by a ballet teacher.

Some might raise the objection that there is no sense of divine call in this story. However, this course is based on the view that 'calling' is part of the way in which God has made all humanity. We can see this, for example, in our love of beauty and desire for justice. While the response to God's personal call is lacking in the film, the dynamics of discovering and giving expression to a calling are richly evident.

Using this film also shows that Christians can learn from those outside the faith. This view also lies behind the 'Start a conversation' option in the *Practise!* section at the end of each session.

>>Apply within (10 minutes)

This is the opportunity to apply the insights gained from the session to our unique experiences of life. Some will find it helpful to talk through what they have learned while others need time to digest it all. Avoid pressurizing people at this point: they may benefit most simply by listening to others.

The leader and/or group need to decide whether this will be done in one group, or by working in pairs and triplets. Generally, working in smaller groups is better because everyone gets to contribute and it is easier to share from our own experience in a group of two or three. It does not have to be done the same way in every session.

>>Pray (5 minutes)

This exercise acts like a Collect because it collects up our thoughts, experiences and responses to the session in prayer to God. This is another appropriate element to ask someone to handle for the group. See guidelines in the opening prayer section above.

>>Practise! (5 minutes)

This is a vital part of the session when people agree to practise in the time before the next session some aspect of what the group has explored together.

> Give people the chance to look at the suggestions.

> Invite them to say what they would like to do.

> Ask people to be ready to report back at the next session their successes and struggles.

It is fine for several people to do the same thing. Although the norm would be for anyone to do one of the options, there is no reason why they cannot do more – if they wish.

A note on the final session: As a conclusion to the course, participants are invited to develop a personal action plan (see pages 66–67).

>>Resources

Background reading

This course draws particularly on:

Francis Dewar, *Live for a Change*, Darton, Longman & Todd, 1988

Francis Dewar, *Invitations*, SPCK, 1996

Gerard Hughes, *God of Surprises*, Darton, Longman & Todd, 1985

Other books referred to or drawn upon are:

David Ford, *The Shape of Living*, HarperCollins 1997

Timothy Radcliffe, *What is the Point of Being a Christian?*,
    Burns & Oates, 2005

Christina Rees, *The Divine Embrace*, Darton, Longman & Todd, 2006

Rick Warren, *The Purpose Driven Life*, Zondervan, 2002

Dallas Willard, *In Search of Guidance*, Zondervan, 1993

Other books on whole-life calling

John Adair, *How to Find your Vocation*, Canterbury Press, 2002

Bruce Bugbee, *What You Do Best in the Body of Christ: Discover your spiritual gifts, personal style and God-given passion*, Zondervan, 2005

Mark Greene, *Thank God it's Monday*, Scripture Union Publishing, 2002

Mark Greene (ed.), *Pocket Prayers for Work*,
Church House Publishing, 2004
Diana and Lawrence Osborn, *God's Diverse People*,
Darton, Longman & Todd, 1991
Peter C. Wagner, *Discover your Spiritual Gifts*, Regal Books, 2005

Also see the Vocations Sunday web site:
www.cofe-ministry.org.uk/vocsun

Films

Billy Elliot (2000, Certificate 15, Director – Stephen Daldry)
The Lion, the Witch and the Wardrobe (2005, Certificate PG,
Director – Andrew Adamson)
Chariots of Fire (1981, Certificate U, Director – Hugh Hudson)

Music

As an aid to the prayer elements:

> **Taizé** CDs, such as *Wait for the Lord* (Gia, 1995)

> **Instrumental Praise** series of CDs (Brentwood, 1999)

> **Smooth Classics** (Classic FM, 2002)

> **Moon, Sun and All Things** (Hyperion, 2005), especially track 16, 'Dulce Jesús mío'

> **Global Journey** (North Star Music, 1996)

> **Chillout Worship 2004** (Authentic Music)

Images

If you want to use images of Christ as a visual focus, try:

> **The Christ We Share** pack (CMS/USPG), which contains over 30 images of Christ.

> **Icon postcards** – many cathedrals, churches or religious bookshops sell postcard images.

> **www.google.co.uk** – click on Images then enter Christ, icons of Christ, Christ healing, Christ teaching, Christ praying, contemporary Christ.

> **www.rejesus.co.uk** contains many images of Jesus, including some 'unexpected faces'.

>>What's on the Life Calling web link

Go to **www.chpublishing.co.uk/lifecalling** for downloads of the following:

> The course prayer

> The Methodist Covenant Prayer

> Psalms to be used in session 3 (see p. 39) and session 4 (p. 49)

> Appendix 1: Discovering God's call

> Appendix 2: Mrs Fidget handout

> Worship ideas for Vocations Sunday or another service celebrating vocation

>>Aim

This introductory session explores what it means to live out of a sense of call from God.

What you will need (make your own selection)

> Journal for each participant (or ask them to buy their own for the next session);

> Resources for the prayer elements (see p. 9);

> DVD of the film *Billy Elliot*.

>>Background

Leaders: For tips on making the most of the background material, see p. 6.

We live in a frantic world where all too easily we are chasing our tails and trying to pack a vast amount into our lives. This is due in part to the explosion of communications (Internet, budget airlines, etc.), our earning power (enabling us to have a great array of possessions), and to the choices open to us (24/7 shopping, online services, video and DVD entertainment options). We can end up trapped by the pressure of the immediate and feel we have no time to stop and reflect on what really matters.

This session explores what it means to live life out of a sense of call from God and the blessings that come from doing so.

What does it mean to be called?

The word 'vocation' stems from the Latin verb *vocare*, meaning 'to call'. The idea of vocation as a calling from God reverberates throughout the Scriptures. In the New Testament, the Greek verb *kalein* means 'to call'. It has four elements that express the richness of God's calling.

1. The most common use of *kalein* is **to call a person by name**. In Matthew 1.21, the angel of the Lord tells Joseph that they are to *call* their son 'Jesus'. When God reveals himself to Moses at the burning bush he simply says: 'Moses, Moses'. Likewise, when God *calls* Samuel, he addresses him by name. God's *call* is to a personal relationship with him in which he makes himself and his will known to us. **God's call is personal.**

2. Another usage of the verb *kalein* is **to invite a person to a meal or celebration**. It is used in the Parable of the Banquet (Matthew 22.3) for *inviting* the guests to the wedding feast. It is the word used to *invite* those called to the great celebration at the end of time (Revelation 19.9) and the word Luke uses to describe how to behave when *invited* to a wedding banquet (Luke 14.8). Being called by God means being invited and welcomed to enjoy God's hospitality and friendship. It is a call that rests, not on our achievements or merits, but on the loving goodness of God. It is a gift before it is a duty. **God calls us to celebrate.**

   Our vocation, or call from God, is not – in the first place – about *doing* anything. It is a call to be myself in relationship with God and to celebrate his company and generosity and the wonder and beauty of all that is. It is a call to *be*, before it is a call to *do* anything.

3. *Kalein* is also used to indicate that **a person is summoned to an office or an honour**; summoned to a particular position. Paul regards himself as *called* to the office of an apostle (Romans 1.1). In the Parable of the Talents (Matthew 25.14) the servants are *called* to take care of the owner's property. Similarly, in the Parable of the Labourers in the Vineyard (Matthew 20.8) the owner *calls* his workers to give them their reward for their work. Being called by God means being called to a task, a service in the world. **God calls us to action.**

4. Finally, *kalein* is used in the New Testament when **a person is summoned to give an account** or even to stand trial. It is the verb used when Paul is *summoned* before Felix the governor to answer his accusers. Similarly, the verb is used when Peter and John are *required to appear* before a religious court (Acts 4.18).

Ultimately, we are all called to give an account before God of how we have responded to his call. **God calls us to account.**

Bible passage background: Abraham's call (Genesis 17.1-7)

God's encounter with Abram here is a continuation of a calling that began much earlier. Our calling too is ongoing: what God calls us to today is connected to our history with God and deeply linked to who we are.

> **Abram's calling is personal and particular to him.** He is named and known by God. The fact that God gives him a new name is profoundly important since, in the Old Testament, names express a person's character and destiny. His new name defines his call to be the 'father of nations'. Note too that the name change involves the insertion of the first syllable of Yahweh into the middle of Abram's name. This is a call to give expression to God's nature in the way he handles his life.

> **Abraham's calling is a cause for celebration.** A couple, well past the age of childbearing, are promised multitudes of descendants (vv. 15-16). It is little wonder that, when Sarah heard the news, she burst out laughing (Genesis 18.12)! But with God all things are possible. As we consider our own vocation we need to bear this in mind. The celebration extends far beyond the lives of the individuals, Sarah and Abraham; it flows outwards and through the generations in God's eternal promise 'to be God to you and to your offspring after you' (v. 7). Following God's calling has an individual and corporate dimension.

> **Abraham's rich blessing from God involves a summons to action.** The covenant involves two parties. God outlines his side of the promise only after he has outlined to Abraham his responsibilities, for which he will be called to account: 'walk before me and be blameless' (v. 1). Abraham's work is to trust in the promise and to adopt a God-centred attitude, sharing in God's eternal purposes in the world. Abraham's response is to fall on his face before the living God (v. 3).

> **Essential to the fulfilment of Abraham's vocation are his humility and willingness to listen.** It is no different for us.

>> 1 Called by God/The Session

>>Welcome (5 minutes)

Make sure members of the group know each other's names.
If this is a new group meeting for the first time, invite members
of the group to introduce themselves or one another.

This introductory session explores what it means to live out of a sense of
call from God rather than letting life run us.

>>Pray (5–10 minutes)

**The practice of wonder is a good way to be aware of
God's goodness and loving purposes for all creation and
for us his creatures. It helps us to be open to his purposes in
our lives.**

Create a still atmosphere. You might like to read out the hymn
'For the beauty of the earth' (*Hymns for Today's Church* 298; *Common
Praise* 253), play Louis Armstrong's 'What a wonderful world' (widely
available on CD) or another piece of reflective music, or use a picture or
video of some natural beauty.

Be still and recall before God those things and experiences that fill you
with a sense of awe, wonder and delight.

Offer them with thanksgiving to God
(silently or in a word or phrase spoken out loud).

Say together the course prayer:

> **Eternal God,**
> **the light of the minds that know you,**
> **the joy of the hearts that love you,**
> **and strength of the wills that serve you:**

grant us so to know you
    that we may truly love you,
and so to love you
that we may truly serve you,
whose service is perfect freedom;
through Jesus Christ our Lord. Amen.

after St Augustine of Hippo, AD *430*

>>Time to share (5 minutes)

Use the following quotations to help you reflect on the
questions below. Work either as a whole group or in pairs.

The search for the purpose of life
has puzzled people for thousands of years.
That's because we typically begin
at the wrong starting point – ourselves . . .
If you want to know why you were placed on this planet,
you must begin with God.

Rick Warren, The Purpose Driven Life, *p. 17*

Humanity is created to praise, reverence and serve God . . .

Ignatius Loyola, Spiritual Exercises

> In what ways have we found this to be true in our experience?

> Have we seen this God-centred perspective at work in the lives
of others we know or whose stories we have read?

>>Encounter (20–25 minutes)

a. Input: the nature of God's call

(5–10 minutes)

Leader: Using the background information on p. 17, give a brief
introduction to the meaning of calling in the Bible.

b. Read about the call of Abraham (5 minutes)
The call of Abraham (Genesis 17.1-7, NRSV)

[1] When Abram was ninety-nine years old, the Lord appeared to Abram, and said to him, 'I am God Almighty; walk before me, and be blameless. [2] And I will make my covenant between me and you, and will make you exceedingly numerous.' [3] Then Abram fell on his face; and God said to him, [4] 'As for me, this is my covenant with you: You shall be the ancestor of a multitude of nations. [5] No longer shall your name be Abram, but your name shall be Abraham; for I have made you the ancestor of a multitude of nations. [6] I will make you exceedingly fruitful; and I will make nations of you, and kings shall come from you. [7] I will establish my covenant between me and you, and your offspring after you throughout their generations, for an everlasting covenant, to be God to you and to your offspring after you.

c. Talk about it (10 minutes)

1. Abraham's encounter with God recounted in Genesis 17 is a continuation of a calling that began much earlier.
Read 12.1-4. What does Abraham have to do to respond to God's call?

2. Read Abraham's response to God in Genesis 15.2-3. Discuss how his response differs in this passage.

3. Who is affected by God's calling of Abraham?

>>Do something (20 minutes)

Try one of the following options:
1. Watch a clip from the film *Billy Elliot*. Introduce the extract with the following information:

   Billy Elliot *tells the story of eleven-year-old Billy, who discovers an innate gift for dance that is fostered and developed by a local ballet teacher. The discovery of this gift transforms his life and the life of those around him.*

   Watch the opening sequence of the film, Chapter 1 (0:00:39 to 0:02:26), 'Called to dance'. Do you think that God calls his

people to dance, and sing and paint? Why might he do this?
> Do you think there are any limits to what God might call
people to do?
The lyrics of the song point to an understanding of Billy's
vocation as stretching from womb to tomb. Do you think that
some people might be called to express and develop one
particular gift throughout their lives? Can you think of any
examples of such people?

2. Take a clean sheet of paper/page in your journal.
Draw a 'map' that represents your faith journey. Include on it:
> your earliest experiences of God;
> key moments as you have grown;
> where you are now.

Represent this faith journey in any way you feel appropriate.
There is no 'right' or 'wrong'.

Share your thoughts about your 'map' in pairs.

>>Apply within (10 minutes)

Work together (in pairs or as a whole group) on any one or
more of the following questions:
1. Share any ways in which you have felt a sense of being called by God
to something, or have observed that sense of call in someone else.
How did it come about and what does it have to say to you now?
2. Imagine a perceptive friend who knows you well being asked what they
see you called to be and/or do. What would they say?

>>Pray (5 minutes)
The discipline of giving and receiving

Hearing God's call requires that we let go of our sometimes
tight grip on our plans and open ourselves to God's possibilities.
This prayer exercise helps us do that.

The leader of this exercise invites everyone to:

> put aside books and papers;
> sit upright in their chairs, with both feet on the floor and hands resting on thighs;
> take a few minutes just to relax and breathe slowly.

After a few minutes, the leader should invite those present to place their palms face down. The leader then speaks the following words slowly, phrase by phrase, allowing people space to respond.

Hands down: letting go . . .
the tasks, goals, and pressures of our life at present . . .
the demands and expectations that weigh us down . . .
anything we are anxious about . . .
Place them in the hands of the God who has told us to cast all our anxieties on him because he cares for us (1 Peter 5.7).

Hands up: taking hold . . .
'See' God putting into our lives the good gifts of . . .
his presence . . .
his gifts and insights to fulfil our calling . . .
his invitation to join with him in his loving purposes for all that he has created . . .
We can do so with confidence because he has said that his yoke is easy and his burden is light (Matthew 11.30).

Be still:
Stay in God's presence: enjoy his welcome . . .
'Our Father in heaven' *(the leader repeats this short phrase, not the whole prayer slowly, several times).*

The leader brings the period of silence to a close with the words, 'the kingdom, the power, and the glory are yours now and for ever. Amen.'

>>Practise! (5 minutes)

Decide which of the following ideas you wish to try before the next session. Be prepared to report back on your experience.

Journal reflection:

Read the following words slowly, watching out for connections with your own experience.

For most people . . . the calling of God seems to be breathed into their lives as their lives unfold. They are drawn to certain things at certain times, and the necessary doors swing open. They rarely know exactly what they are meant to achieve, but they often have the sense that they are where they should be . . .

I can best describe my own sense of calling as a sense of obedience. I am aware that I can obey God, or not, and if I were to abandon what I am doing, or even change the focus, I would feel as if I were disobeying God . . . Sometimes, the positive, feel-good factor is completely absent, and all I have to go on is this sense of obedience, that I am following where someone else is guiding . . .

Being called gives purpose, vision and strength, but not always an overall or detailed view of how things will unfold.

Christina Rees, The Divine Embrace: Discovering the reality of God's love, *pp. 101–102*

Take time to copy this passage into your journal. Write slowly and meditatively. Underline any particular words or phrases that hold your attention for whatever reason. Write a prayer to God in which you express your thoughts and feelings about this passage.

Talk with a friend/prayer partner about:

> the above quotation and the issues it raises for you;

> what you are noticing about your calling in every aspect of your life;

> about the questions in *Apply within*, above.

Practise the spiritual discipline of giving and receiving:

> letting go of pressures, burdens, expectations and worries;

> letting God in on the tasks that trouble you and the ones you are enthusiastic about and seeking an understanding of how he calls you to approach them;

> receiving God's good plans on trust – even before you know them.

Keep a watch: when viewing TV, reading newspapers or magazines, keep an ear/eye open for comments people make about their sense of call. Make a note in your journal and share with the group at the next session.

Start a conversation: with someone outside the membership of the church about their sense of call and how it came about. Be honest in sharing your story. Expect to learn from them.

>> 2 Called from within/Beforehand

>>Aim

The aim of this session is to explore what it means to be made in God's image – and the implication for our life calling.

What you will need (make your own selection)

> Journal for each participant;

> Resources for prayer elements;

> Use of a picture of the heavens would fit well in this session;

> DVD of the film *Billy Elliot*.

>>Background

Leaders: for tips on using this background material, see p. 6.

Where does vocation come from? Is it from outside us, from God; or does it arise from within us?

Dictionaries give us interesting answers here, for language is a living reality that reflects changes taking place in society. *The Shorter Oxford English Dictionary* (1933) has three definitions. Two refer to God calling someone and another to an ecclesiastical body doing the calling. The emphasis in all three is on someone external to the self, giving a call to a particular work.

More recently, the *Longman Dictionary of Contemporary English* (1987) shows a striking change. It also has three definitions. Here, however, the focus in the first two is on a 'particular fitness or ability' to do something. Only the third refers to a source outside the person.

Life Calling sees these two understandings as two sides of the same coin. God's call is from beyond us yet sparks into life what is within us. This session looks first at the external source, namely our being created in God's image (Genesis 1), and then explores how we can get in touch with our personal call by identifying our inner longings, passions and 'holy desires'.

What are the implications of being made in God's image?

> **We are called to *love*.** This is a call to receive God's love and to give ourselves in love to him. From this source, love flows towards all creation, and all humanity in its diversity; those closest to us as well as those far away.

> **We are called to be *creative*.** We see this in a child's capacity to play and in an adult's longing for fulfilling work and desire to 'make something of my life'. This call to creativity is not limited to paid employment but is an instinct deep within us to bring good things into being, whether another human life, a work of art, a sport or physical activity, a service to others, a human organization or 'a better world'. Like Jesus in Joseph's carpenter's shop, we are called to be co-workers and to share in our Father's creative work. This is the active, doing, aspect to our being living images: not least because God is a God who acts.

> **We are called to *serve*.** This is not about a servile attitude. Rather it is about making connections between our life and God's loving purposes for his world. It was for this that Christ came and his kingdom is at work, overcoming evil with good and working to bring wholeness into every situation. Cooperating with this divine agenda is the vocation of all believers. How it happens is unique to each one. In discerning our particular calling we need to remember that mission is not something we do for God, but something God is doing and in which he calls us to share.

> **We are called to *rest*, *reflect* and *rejoice*.** The Sabbath command is the only one God is specifically recorded as practising (Genesis 2.2). In today's frantic culture we need to stop and reflect on life, enjoy the good, and recognize that we are human beings not just human doings. Rest and reflection are essential if we are to avoid the weariness that comes from trying to save the world, the distraction of too many demands and the danger of taking ourselves too seriously.

Each of these aspects of our calling to be living images of a loving God gives shape to our vocation. Most of us experience an unfolding and developing call related to different phases of life. For some this sense of direction in life comes early on and shapes the whole of our living. For others, it is more like the manna in the wilderness: we receive enough – freshly given – for each stage of the journey. Seeking to discern the shape of that calling brings order, peace and purpose to our living.

Bible passage background: God's creation of humankind (Genesis 1.26-31)

Our passage begins with God speaking, 'Let us make humankind in our image.' The pronouns God uses indicate a profound truth: God is relational. Relationship to the other is at the heart of God's being. Made in God's likeness, we are called to reflect that through our relationship with God and others. At the heart of such relationship is *love*.

Genesis 1 portrays the vastness of God's *creativity* as he speaks the heavens and the earth into existence. Light comes into being, water springs forth and growth begins. At the crescendo of this creativity, humanity is fashioned. Made in God's image and likeness, we are called to reflect that creativity, bringing into being life in the widest sense.

God orders humanity to 'have dominion'. This does not mean bullying domination, but rather calls for relationship to creation that reflects God's care for all, from the great beasts to the 'creeping things', to say nothing of other human beings. The hallmark of God's mission is generous *service*.

In verse 31, God looks upon all creation and is delighted by it. Satisfied with his labours, God *rests*. Part of our calling is simply to stop, enjoy God and life, and reflect on that and the world around us.

>>Welcome (5 minutes)

Welcome people back to the group. The aim of this session is to explore what we are called to do as a result of being made in God's image.

>>Pray (5–10 minutes)

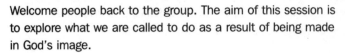

We are not good at being still. Even when we 'relax' we end up doing something: reading, watching TV, planning the shopping list or our next holiday. Being in touch with God – and our deepest desires – requires the discipline of stillness. It cannot be achieved in one five-minute exercise in a group, but doing just that can help us to get going – in the matter of stopping!

Create a still atmosphere, for example by lighting a candle.

Put papers aside and let someone lead the group through the following stages, reading or paraphrasing the words in italics below. Allow at least one minute for each of the last four steps.

1. **Sit well.** Hold your spine and head erect, with your hands loosely on your lap, and your feet flat on the floor.

2. **Be still.** Let your mind become still. If any distractions surface, acknowledge them and return to stillness.

3. **Be aware** – of your body, starting with your toes and moving up to your face and head. This is not a medical check-up but a way of being quietly aware of your own body.

4. **Listen.** Listen to any sounds; do not work out where they are coming from, but pay attention to the quality of the sounds themselves.

5. **Look.** Choose some object around you and let it have your full attention – its shape, colour, texture, and so on. If it provokes interesting thoughts, acknowledge them and bring yourself back to simply looking.

Leader says, (slowly, giving time between each line):

> Be still and know that I am God . . .
> Be still and know that I am . . .
> Be still and know . . .
> Be still . . .
> Be . . .

And/or end with the course prayer:

> **Eternal God,**
> **the light of the minds that know you,**
> **the joy of the hearts that love you,**
> **and strength of the wills that serve you:**
> **grant us so to know you**
> > **that we may truly love you,**
> **and so to love you**
> **that we may truly serve you,**
> **whose service is perfect freedom;**
> **through Jesus Christ our Lord. Amen.**
> > > > *after St Augustine of Hippo,* AD *430*

>>Action replay (5 minutes)

Invite group members to talk about the practice they agreed to do last week. Encourage people to share snippets from their journals if appropriate.

>>Time to share (5 minutes)

Use the following quotations to help you reflect on the questions below. Work either as a whole group or in pairs.

The glory of God is a human being fully alive.

St Irenaeus

Our chief end is to glorify God and enjoy him for ever.

The Westminster Catechism

> In what ways has this been true in our experience of life?

> Where have we seen these principles at work in the lives of others we know or whose stories we have read?

>>Encounter (20–25 minutes)

a. Input: being living images of God
(5 minutes)

Leader: using the background material on p. 26, give a brief introduction to what it means to be a living image of God.

b. Read about God's creation of humankind
(5 minutes)

God's creation of humankind (Genesis 1.26 – 2.2)

[1.26] Then God said, 'Let us make humankind in our image, according to our likeness; and let them have dominion over the fish of the sea, and over the birds of the air, and over the cattle, and over all the wild animals of the earth, and over every creeping thing that creeps upon the earth.'

[27] So God created humankind in his image, in the image of God he created them; male and female he created them.

[28] God blessed them, and God said to them, 'Be fruitful and multiply, and fill the earth and subdue it; and have dominion over the fish of the sea and over the birds of the air and over every living thing that moves upon the earth.' [29] God said, 'See, I have given you every plant yielding seed that is upon the face of all the earth, and every tree with seed in its fruit; you shall have them for food. [30] And to every beast of the earth, and to every bird of the air, and to everything that creeps on the earth, everything that has the breath of life, I have given every green plant for food.' And it was so. [31] God saw everything that he had made, and indeed, it was

very good. And there was evening and there was morning, the sixth day.

2.1 Thus the heavens and the earth were finished, and all their multitude. ² And on the seventh day God finished the work that he had done, and he rested on the seventh day from all the work that he had done. ³ So God blessed the seventh day and hallowed it, because on it God rested from all the work that he had done in creation.

c. Talk about it (15 minutes)

Talk about either of/both these questions.

1. In the light of what we learn about God in this passage, what do you think it means for us to be 'made in the image of God' (Genesis 1.26)?

2. God delights in the result of his work (v. 31): what aspects of your life (including work, leisure, relationships, and concern for the wider world) give you the greatest satisfaction?

>>Do something (20 minutes)

Try one of the following activities:

1. Watch a clip from the film *Billy Elliot*. Introduce the clip with the following information: the local ballet teacher has spotted Billy's talents and offered to teach him. She tells him to bring some items that are special to him to help them get ideas for a dance for his audition.

   Watch the film (from 0:36:40 to 0:41:38).

   > Discuss how Billy brings his past – the joys and the struggles – into the act of creating his audition dance. What does this suggest to you about human creativity?

2. Take a clean sheet of paper/page in your journal. Draw a stick figure in the centre of the page, representing you. Around this figure, draw symbols that represent the different roles, tasks and pastimes you engage with in your daily life. (For example – a pan for cooking, spanner for car repair, pen for writing, etc.)

When you have finished, write down, next to each symbol, words or phrases that express your feelings about each one. Don't worry if you find that the same role inspires negative and positive feelings in you at the same time.

In pairs, share your thoughts.

Adapted from Francis Dewar, Live for a Change, *pp. 6–7*

>>Apply within (10 minutes)

Have you ever had a strong urge to study a certain subject? Have you ever fallen completely in love with some new activity, such as playing a musical instrument or dancing? Are you passionate about dogs, or old people, or broadcasting, or biology? I think it's always worth pursuing your deeply felt interests and seeing where they lead you . . . Listen carefully to what your heart is saying, for it may be whispering where you are to take your next step. Enjoy the process as best you can, trusting that God is always holding you and helping you to become all that you are created to be.

Christina Rees, The Divine Embrace, *p. 110*

Work together on either of/both these questions:

1. What issues has this session raised for you and how might you act on the insights gained?

2. Bearing in mind the above quotation, share together what:

   > gives you the greatest pleasure;

   > represents your deepest longings;

   > you would love to be or do.

>>Pray (5 minutes)

To live out of a sense of call from God requires that we bring our passions, skills and longings before God and allow him to direct how we handle them.

Leader: invites everyone to focus on the wonder of Christ's self-giving love on the cross.

You might like to do this by singing/listening to/reading the first verse of the hymn 'When I survey the wondrous cross' (*Hymns for Today's Church* 147; *Common Praise* 127), or of 'My song is love unknown' (*Hymns for Today's Church* 136; *Common Praise* 112).

Then invite all in silence, out loud, or both, to name before God the passions that inspired Christ's living and his Passion, such as his love for all, his desire to do the Father's will, etc.

Gather up your praise by one person reading (or by everyone singing) the final verse of the hymn you have chosen.

Invite everyone (in silence) to offer to God our skills, our longings and our tightly held plans – for him to direct and bless as he wills.

Conclude by praying together:

> **Almighty God,**
> **who wonderfully created us in your own image**
> **and yet more wonderfully restored us**
> **through your Son Jesus Christ:**
> **grant that, as he came to share in our humanity,**
> **so we may share the life of his divinity;**
> **who is alive and reigns with you,**
> **in the unity of the Holy Spirit,**
> **one God, now and for ever. Amen.**
> *Collect for the First Sunday of Christmas, Common Worship, p. 381*

>>Practise! (5 minutes)

Read through the options here then identify, and share with each other, which one (or more) of these you wish to pursue and report back about at the next session.

Journal reflection:

Read the following words slowly, watching out for connections with your own experience.

If we were able to discover what we really want, if we could become conscious of the deepest desire within us, then we should have discovered God's will. God's will is not an impersonal blueprint for living forced on us by a capricious God and contrary to almost every inclination in us. God's will is our freedom. He wants us to discover what we really want and who we really are. The struggle is not our will against God's will, but our will struggling with its divided self, the will which wants all creation to praise, reverence and serve me against the will which wants to praise, reverence and serve God, the will which wants to take over from God against the will which wants to let God be God.

The saint is the person who has discovered his/her deepest desire. They then 'do their own thing', which is also God's thing. Their will and God's will are in harmony, so that their lives are characterised by a continuous peace, tranquillity, freedom and joy, even – perhaps especially – in crises and suffering.

Gerard Hughes, God of Surprises, *p. 62*

Take time to copy this passage into your journal. Write slowly and meditatively. Underline particular words or phrases that hold your attention. Write a prayer to God in which you express your thoughts and feelings about this passage.

Talk with a friend/prayer partner about:

> the above 'journal' quotation;

> the questions in the *Apply within* section;

> your deepest longings, desires and hopes;

> the issues raised for you by them.

Practise the spiritual discipline of stillness:

> by doing the Stillness exercise from this session, two or three times, and noting joys and struggles;

> by stilling your mind in those stopping moments in life; in the supermarket queue, waiting for the computer to come on or the kettle to boil, waiting for a service or meeting to begin.

Keep a watch: when viewing TV, reading newspapers or magazines, keep an ear/eye open for comments people make about what motivates them. Watch out for ways in which they attribute their focus in life to their own choices or external forces. Make a note in your journal and share with the group at the next session.

Start a conversation: with someone outside the membership of the church about times when they have felt most alive, or what they would say was their calling in different aspects of their life. Be honest in sharing with them what yours are. Expect to learn from them.

>> 3 Called out/Beforehand

>>Aim

To explore how responding to God's call sets us free.

What you will need (make your own selection)

> Journal for each participant;

> Resources for prayer elements;

> DVD of Billy Elliot or The Lion, the Witch and the Wardrobe;

> Download of the Mrs Fidget story (see p. 70).

>>Background

Leaders: For tips on making the most of the background material, see p. 6.

This session looks at the obstacles to our living in response to God's call. These barriers take the form of patterns of living arising from:

> **our upbringing** (need to achieve, desire to please);

> **ways in which we compensate for hurts of the past** (self-defeating attitudes and addictions);

> **our particular personality** (compulsions and instinctual responses to life);

> **the context in which we live/work** (others' demands and expectations);

> **the 'tyranny of the urgent'**, which leaves us chasing our tails, and stifles the creativity and gifts that lie buried within us.

These barriers arise out of our experience of the brokenness of the human predicament. They often involve wrong choices – including wrong responses to negative experiences in life. Wrong choices lead to our having idols that trap who we are and what we do. They are often evidenced in our hiding from God, others, ourselves and reality.

The good news is that God, in Christ and by the Holy Spirit, is able to free us from all that robs us of the fullness of life found in following his way.

Bible passage background: Jesus promises rest (Matthew 11.28-30)

Jesus calls us out of the burdens we lay on ourselves. His promise of freedom from the cycle of weariness comes to all who recognize that they are carrying heavy and exacting burdens. Often, Jesus encounters those who are 'weary and heavy laden' – from those burdened by what they do, by the nature of their employment (Matthew 9.9), to those bound by how they think, by exacting, rigid religious mindsets (Matthew 12.1-8). All are called out from burdens that weigh down, bind and limit, though not all recognize the invitation. To all, Jesus promises rest.

The word 'yoke' (v. 30) is an agricultural term referring to a wooden bar fastened over the necks of two animals and attached to their load. Frequently, we yoke ourselves to unhelpful things in an attempt to pull along various burdens (e.g. low self-esteem or the expectations of others). We may yoke ourselves to (among other things): relationships that are distorted and damaging; obsessive ambition and overwork, which may cost us our health; religious practices that become gods in themselves; or vicious cycles of addiction to food or chemical substances or notions of bodily perfection. Those things to which we have yoked ourselves become our false gods: the things to which we give our time and energy. Jesus calls us out of this idolatry.

In their place Jesus offers the companionship, guidance and encouragement of being yoked to him as we work together to bring about the purposes of God in our world.

Jesus requires active response on our part: to 'take' his yoke and to 'learn' from him. This is a call out of complacency and wilful avoidance; a call to face the truth about the damaging things to which we have yoked ourselves. It is a call to listen to and to trust in one who assures us of a gentle reception, whatever the truth is that we need to confess and from which we need to turn.

The call of Zacchaeus (Luke 19.1-8)

A good example of this active response to the call out of idolatry can be seen in the life of Zacchaeus, the wealthy chief tax collector.

Luke gives us plenty of clues that Zacchaeus is searching for something more than money; perhaps the existence of his wealth and power had become a wearying burden to him. Whatever is driving him is powerful enough for him to leave the office (or 'his tax collecting') and risk encountering a hostile crowd. Climbing a tree to see Jesus underlines his determination and desperation.

Jesus calls Zacchaeus out of the tree, and out of a life yoked to greed. That Zacchaeus is prepared to give half his possessions to the poor and to pay back anyone he has defrauded four times over underlines the truth that he has heard Jesus' call. His response is active and costly: letting go of a grasping lifestyle and choosing generosity instead. He has discovered freedom by being yoked to Christ.

A note on the Apply within exercise

These are personal matters that need sensitive handling, helping each other to find God's freedom, rather than pointing the finger or putting each other right. The leader can help this process by giving a lead in owning what you struggle with, doing so in an appropriate and honest way.

>>Welcome (5 minutes)

Welcome people back to the group. This session is about how God sets us free from all that hinders us from responding to his call.

>>Pray (5–10 minutes)
A psalm of openness to change (Psalm 40.1-8)

Invite someone to read the psalm.

Allow a short pause for extemporary prayer offering ourselves to God for this session, or use the course prayer.

> **Eternal God,**
> **the light of the minds that know you,**
> **the joy of the hearts that love you,**
> **and strength of the wills that serve you:**
> **grant us so to know you**
> **   that we may truly love you,**
> **and so to love you**
> **that we may truly serve you,**
> **whose service is perfect freedom;**
> **through Jesus Christ our Lord. Amen.**

after St Augustine of Hippo, AD *430*

>>Action replay (5 minutes)

Invite group members to share their experiences of undertaking any of the practices agreed at the end of the last session.

>>Time to share (5 minutes)

Use the following quotations to help you reflect on the questions overleaf. Work either as a whole group or in pairs.

Finally, I realized that both for myself and other people, addictions are not limited to substances. I was also addicted to work, performance, responsibility, intimacy, being liked, helping others, and an almost endless list of other behaviours.

Gerard May, Addiction and Grace, *p. 9*

If not to God, you will surrender to the opinions or expectations of others, to money, to resentment, to fear, or to your own pride, lusts or ego. You were designed to worship God – and if you fail to worship him, you will create other things (idols) to give your life to.

Rick Warren, The Purpose Driven Life, *p. 82*

> In what ways have we found this to be true in our experience?
> Where have we seen these principles at work in the lives of others we know or whose stories we have read?

>>Encounter (20–25 minutes)

a. Input: being set free to respond to God's call (5 minutes)

Leader: Using the background information on p. 0, give a brief introduction to some of the obstacles that prevent us from responding to God's call.

b. Read about Jesus' offer of rest and the call of Zacchaeus (5 minutes)
Matthew 11.28-30 (NRSV)

[28] 'Come to me, all you that are weary and are carrying heavy burdens, and I will give you rest. [29] Take my yoke upon you, and learn from me; for I am gentle and humble in heart, and you will find rest for your souls. [30] For my yoke is easy, and my burden is light.'

Luke 19.1-10 (NRSV)

[1] He entered Jericho and was passing through it. [2] A man was there named Zacchaeus; he was a chief tax-collector and was rich. [3] He was trying to see who Jesus was, but on account of the crowd he could not, because he was short in stature. [4] So he ran ahead and climbed a sycamore tree to see him, because he was going to pass that way. [5] When Jesus came to the place, he looked up and said to him, 'Zacchaeus, hurry and come down; for I must stay at your house today.' [6] So he hurried down and was happy to welcome him. [7] All who saw it began to grumble and said, 'He has gone to be the guest of one who is a sinner.' [8] Zacchaeus stood there and said to the Lord, 'Look, half of my possessions, Lord, I will give to the poor; and if I have defrauded anyone of anything, I will pay back four times as much.' [9] Then Jesus said to him, 'Today salvation has come to this house, because he too is a son of Abraham. [10] For the Son of Man came to seek out and to save the lost.'

c. Talk about it (15 minutes)

1. What were the idols and addictions in Zacchaeus's life? What is the evidence that he was able to break free from them?

2. Jesus says, 'Take my yoke upon you and learn from me'. Imagine that a member of the church youth group asked you to explain how you do this. What would your response be?

3. What kinds of heavy burden and wearying behaviour do you think Jesus calls us out of today?

>>Do something (20 minutes)

Try *one* of the following:

1. Watch a clip from the film *Billy Elliot*. Introduce the extract with the following information:

(NB Please note that this clip contains some strong language.)

Finally, Billy Elliot has secured an audition for the Royal Ballet School following a huge change of heart from his father, who was initially opposed to his son's dancing.

Watch the film from chapter 14 (01:19:14), when Billy tells his Dad he has changed his mind, to chapter 15 (01:26:50), when the examiner wishes Mr Elliot good luck with the strike.

> What attitudes and habits will Billy need to leave behind if he is to succeed as a ballet dancer?

2. Watch a clip from the film *The Lion, the Witch and the Wardrobe*.

Introduce the extract with the following information:

The Pevensie children have been evacuated to a remote house. In a game of hide and seek, Lucy discovers the wardrobe that leads into Narnia and meets the fawn Mr Tumnus. On her return, no one believes her, and her brother Edmund is particularly spiteful, even after he discovers the truth about Narnia.

Watch the film from chapter 5 (00:27:00), when Edmund enters the wardrobe, to chapter 7 (00:36:36), when the old man tells them, 'You're a family . . . you might try acting like one.'

> In what ways does the white witch hook Edmund's loyalty? What attitudes and behaviours will Edmund need to leave behind if he is to behave like a loyal member of his family?

3. Read the story of Mrs Fidget (from C. S. Lewis's *The Four Loves* – see Bibliography – or download from **www.chpublishing.co.uk/lifecalling**) and identify what distinguishes a call from an addiction.

>>Apply within (10 minutes)

The Scriptures tell us to confess our sins to one another (James 5.16) – good advice we find difficult to take. Some things are best dealt with between us and God alone; and other things best addressed with one other person (a 'confessor' of some description). However, honesty is good for us and for the building of true community. So, taking any steps we can in that direction, let's share:

1a. things that we find stand in the way of our living in response to God's call.

1b. habits and tendencies we recognize in ourselves that inhibit who we could be and what we could do.

1c. obstacles in us as a church community that hold us back from living fully out of sense of call from God.

Or consider together:

2. What issues has this session raised for you and what steps can you take to act on the insights gained?

>>Pray (5 minutes)
The discipline of confession

Hearing God's call requires that we let go of our drivenness, and idols, and all that blocks our response to God's will.

Let us reflect on what has been said (or avoided) in the session and seek Christ's forgiveness and freedom.

The Leader takes the group through the following:

Sit upright, relax and breathe slowly. Put both feet on the floor and rest your hands on your thighs. Start with your palms facing down.

Hands down: *letting go of our burdens . . .*
> The attitudes, drives and needs that block our doing God's will . . .
> The need to achieve, please, possess, succeed that gets in the way of responding to God's call . . .
> The urgent that so easily obscures the important things in life . . .

Place them in God's hands – he has promised to take our burdens.

Hands up: *taking hold of Christ's yoke . . .*
'See' God, in Christ, linking you into . . .
> his presence, gifts and insights . . .
> his invitation to join with him in his loving purposes for all . . .

We can do so with confidence because he has said that his yoke is easy and his burden is light (Matthew 11.30).

Be still: pause for a moment of quiet reflection . . .

Closing prayer:

> O God our disturber,
> whose speech is pregnant with power
> and whose word will be fulfilled:
> may we know ourselves unsatisfied
> with all that distorts your truth,
> and make our hearts attentive
> to your liberating voice,
> in Jesus Christ. Amen.
>
> *Janet Morley,* All Desires Known, *p. 17*

>>Practise! (5 minutes)

Look at the following ideas and decide which one you wish to pursue and report back on at the next session.

Journal reflection:

> Read the following words slowly, watching out for connections with your own experience.

Having to die in order to live may not make sense to everyone, but it will make sense to everyone who has ever had to give up cherished hopes and dreams, only to have them returned later, refined, more realistic and at exactly the right time. Sometimes dreams don't come back, but others do, dreams you could not have imagined before. For some, the biggest death will be to their own sense of being in control; for others, it will mean death to a certain view of yourself that has no part in the reality of God's love. But all the deaths and dying will lead to new life, new discoveries, new hopes and new vision. And through all the dying, God calls, reaching out to all people, and those who hear the call and respond become the means by which God continues to call others.

Christina Rees, The Divine Embrace, *p. 112*

Take time to copy this passage into your journal. Write slowly and meditatively. Underline any particular words or phrases that hold your attention.

Write a prayer to God asking for forgiveness and freedom.

Talk with a friend/prayer partner about:

> the above quotation and the issues it raises for you;
> any way in which you are aware of allowing drives such as those identified in the Rick Warren quote (p. 40) to inhibit your response to God's call.

Practise the spiritual discipline of confession:

> Each night, say 'thank you' to God for something good about the day, say 'sorry' for something you regret, and 'please' for some way of dealing with that wrong.
> Check out your sins. Is what you confess really a sin – namely a distortion of the character of God – or a put-down of yourself, or simply loss of face?
> Practise making a double confession. First, confess your sin to God; then confess that Christ has forgiven you fully.

Keep a watch: when viewing TV, reading newspapers or magazines, keep an ear/eye open for comments people make about what motivates them or where their motivation comes from. What do people talk about being driven by? Make a note in your journal and share with the group at the next session.

Start a conversation: with someone outside the membership of the church about times and ways in which they feel driven by life, events and the expectations of others. Be honest in sharing with them what yours are. Expect to learn from them.

>> 4 Called up/Beforehand

>>Aim

To explore what it means to be called up into Christ's mission on earth.

What you will need (make your own selection)

> Journal for all;

> DVD of the film *Chariots of Fire*;

> Scissors, glue, large pieces of paper, pens, range of recent newspapers.

Background

Leaders: for tips on making the most of the background material, see p. 6.

'Doing your own thing' is our culture's starting point in its approach to life. This session explores the richer and more ancient wisdom of the gospel, enshrined in the famous dictum of St Augustine, that God's service is perfect freedom. Discovering our part in God's purposes is a life-giving and fulfilling call, costly though it may be. A football coach choosing someone to play in the team is an apt contemporary image. The player sees being chosen to play not as constraint on personal freedom, but rather as an affirmation of his or her skills and a great opportunity to use them to the full.

And the goal of Christian service? To play our part in God's loving purposes for all that he has created.

There are many ways in which we can discover our call into the work of God's kingdom. Some of those ways are:

> **turning outwards:** paying attention to the world around us is the basic way to discover what God is calling us to be engaged with. This includes paying attention to the world beyond the life of the church.

> **anger:** rightly handled is 'energy for life' expressing an unwillingness to accept the broken and distorted. Development agencies report that many people working in tough situations around the world are motivated by anger.

> **grief:** many great pieces of work have come into being as a result of someone daring to stay with grief until it bears fruit. Samaritans, the Hospice Movement and Cruse (bereavement agency) came into being this way. When we say 'something ought to be done about that' we may be planting a seed of vocation in our own hearts!

> **grace:** as those who have received 'grace upon grace', believers are motivated to give out of the riches they have received. Grace draws our attention to where we can give. Though fewer than 10 per cent of people in the UK go to church, over 30 per cent of those involved in local voluntary work are churchgoers. Looking for opportunities to serve is an instinctive response to life for those who follow Christ.

> **what is to hand:** God's call is often found in the 'ordinariness' of life, and in the way we respond to the opportunities, responsibilities and constraints presented to us by them. David overcame Goliath with pebbles he found at his feet. The Hebrew midwives chose to respond in a godly yet costly way in their ordinary daily work.

> **the negative way:** 'If you run out of water, stop rowing'. Sometimes we can discover God's call only by stopping what we realize is no longer part of his purpose for us. Such stopping needs to be done responsibly, often handing over what we have been doing to someone else. It can feel risky as it involves letting go of the security of our role, and feeling exposed without it, before we can discover the new direction.

> **prayer:** not only in the sense of seeking the guidance of God, but also in terms of offering ourselves, our day, and the tasks in front of us to God. Just as Brother Lawrence (see Bibliography) learned prayerfully to pick up a piece of straw from the kitchen floor 'to the glory of God' so we, by connecting 'the daily round, the common task' with the loving

purposes of God, can discover God's call in the midst of the ordinariness of life.

Bible passage background: The Hebrew midwives (Exodus 1.15-21)

At the beginning of Exodus, in the midst of a story of despotic power wielded by a nameless king, we stumble across two women, Hebrew midwives named Shiphrah and Puah. For these women, the call of God arises within the context of their everyday working lives. As midwives, their vocation is to work in cooperation with the God who brings new life into being. Their calling is a loving, creative, serving work: a vocation expressed through their knowledge, wisdom and practice in delivering babies safely. The king, determined to get rid of the descendants of Jacob, tries to enlist their support, ordering them to kill all the Hebrew males at birth.

Shiphrah and Puah's behaviour is governed by the fact that they 'feared God'. They revere the sovereignty of the God who is creator, refusing to be drawn aside by one who is operating as a dealer of death. There is no sense here that God intervenes in a direct manner, calling the midwives to act in accordance with his laws. Rather, they do so because they are attuned to the call of God embedded in their daily living; theirs is a natural, though costly, response to this call.

These women do what they can, with the resources they have, in the situation in which they find themselves. They use what comes to hand: their knowledge of midwifery, which they play off against the king's ignorance. In so doing they are responding to the call of God arising in the ordinariness of their working life.

Although these women are not well known members of society, leaders or policy makers, they have a profound effect on the future of their people. Their faith is seen in their actions, as a result of which Moses is spared at birth. The fulfilment of God's purposes requires the faithfulness of all God's people, regardless of worldly status or position.

>> 4 Called up/The Session

>>Welcome (5 minutes)

Welcome people back to the group. This session explores ways in which we are called to engage with God's work in the world.

>>Pray (5–10 minutes)

See *Introduction* p. 9.

A psalm of God's call to all humanity (Psalm 8)

Invite someone to read the psalm or download the text from **www.chpublishing.co.uk/lifecalling** and produce enough copies for everyone to say it together (alternate verses by men/women, two halves of the room or leader/group).

Pause for prayer: offering ourselves to God for this session.

Close by praying together the course prayer:

> **Eternal God,**
> **the light of the minds that know you,**
> **the joy of the hearts that love you,**
> **and strength of the wills that serve you:**
> **grant us so to know you**
> **that we may truly love you,**
> **and so to love you**
> **that we may truly serve you,**
> **whose service is perfect freedom;**
> **through Jesus Christ our Lord. Amen.**
>
> *after St Augustine of Hippo, AD 430*

>>Action replay (5 minutes)

Invite group members to talk about the practice they agreed to do last week.

Encourage people to share snippets from their journals if appropriate.

>>Time to share (5 minutes)

Use the following quotations to help you reflect on the
questions below. Work either as a whole group or in pairs.

This is the true joy of life:
the being used up for a purpose recognised by yourself
as a mighty one;
being a force of nature
instead of a feverish, selfish little clot of ailments and grievances,
complaining that the world will not devote itself
to making you happy.

George Bernard Shaw, Man and Superman, *p. 33*

No man is happy until he has a cause worth dying for.

Jean-Paul Sartre

What do these quotations, both from atheists, tell us about the way to a
fulfilled life?

>>Encounter (20–25 minutes)

a. Input: being co-workers in God's world
(5–10 minutes)

Leader: using the background information on pp. 46–8, give a brief
introduction to how we can discover our call to be involved in God's work
in the world.

Something to think about . . .

On vocation

To participate in mission is to
participate in the movement of God's love towards people,
since God is a fountain of sending love.

David Bosch, Transforming Mission, *p. 390*

On turning outwards

We come to know even ourselves,
not through turning inward, but by turning outward
to love all that is real and other than ourselves.

Leanne Payne, The Healing Presence, *p. 163*

On anger

Charles Péguy, the French writer, told the story of a man
who died and went to heaven.
When he met the recording angel, he was asked,
'Show me your wounds.'
And he replied, 'Wounds? I have not got any.'
And the angel said,
'Did you never think that anything was worth fighting for?'

Timothy Radcliffe, What is the Point of Being a Christian? *p. 75*

On grief

A Christian is someone who shares
the sufferings of God in the world.

Dietrich Bonhoeffer

---

b. Read about the vocation of the Hebrew midwives
(5 minutes)
Exodus 1.15-21 (NRSV)

[15] The king of Egypt said to the Hebrew midwives, one of whom was named Shiphrah and the other Puah, [16] 'When you act as midwives to the Hebrew women, and see them on the birthstool, if it is a boy, kill him; but if it is a girl, she shall live.' [17] But the midwives feared God; they did not do as the king of Egypt commanded them, but they let the boys live. [18] So the king of Egypt summoned the midwives and said to them, 'Why have you done this, and allowed the boys to live?' [19] The midwives said to Pharaoh, 'Because the Hebrew women are not like the Egyptian women; for they are vigorous and give birth before the midwife comes to them.' [20] So God dealt well with the midwives; and the people multiplied and became very strong. [21] And because the midwives feared God, he gave them families.

c. Talk about it (10 minutes)

1. In what ways do the actions of Shiphrah and Puah, connect with God's purposes?

2. Frequently, in the Scriptures, God's calling comes with the assurance, 'Do not be afraid'. What do you think Shiphrah and Puah might have been afraid of, and how might they have faced and overcome those fears?

3. In pursuing their vocation, the midwives engage in an act of political disobedience. Can you think of more contemporary examples in which a person/people have been forced into acts of disobedience in order to be true to their calling?

4. When you consider God's call in your life, what are you afraid of and why? How might you confront your fears?

>>Do something (20 minutes)

1. Watch three linked clips from the film *Chariots of Fire*. (It is worth looking at all three, but if time is short, look at either the first one or the second two.)

Introduce the first extract with the following:

The film tells the story of Eric Liddell, a missionary and a talented runner, who works hard to balance his gift as a runner and his calling to be a missionary.

Watch the film from chapter 4 (00:22:45), when his senior colleague says, 'You're a very lucky young man, Eric . . .' to chapter 4 (00:26:18), when Eric says, 'Cheers. Thanks for coming, thanks for coming.'

> How effectively do you think Eric uses his gift as a runner 'to the glory of God'?

Introduce the second clip with the following:

Eric has qualified for the 1924 Olympic Games, but the heat for his 100 m race is scheduled for a Sunday. Watch the clip and consider how Eric reacts to the situation.

Watch the film from chapter 17 (01:24:00), when an Olympic official says, 'Lord Birkenhead has advised us . . .' to (01:28:55) when his friend reads from the paper, 'Man of Principle . . .'

> Discuss how Eric holds true to his Christian conviction in the face of considerable pressure to put his talents as a runner before his desire to serve God.

Introduce the third clip with the following:
Eric runs in the 400 m quarter final and qualifies for the final, which we see in this clip.

See chapter 21 (01:48:45), when an American athlete gives Eric a note, to (01:50:50), when Eric is carried on his team mates' shoulders.

> Discuss the deep connection between Eric's call to be a missionary and his gift at running.

2. Prayer tree: Play some quiet music as people engage with this activity (see page 13 for suggestions). In groups of two or three, draw the outline of a tree on a large piece of paper. Give people a range of the day's newspapers. Ask them to flick through and cut out any images/headlines that arouse their anger, grief or compassion. Stick these cut-outs on the tree. Underneath each one, write a one-line prayer concerning the situation.

>>Apply within (10 minutes)

Work together on any of the following questions, possibly in groups of two or three, with each person deciding which question they want to explore with others.

1. What are the issues raised for you by this session and what steps can you see to take to act on the insights gained?

2. What do you see as the main focus of your living at present; and how do you see that connecting with God's purposes and the coming of his kingdom?

3. Think back to the Hebrew midwives. Where might God be
   calling you to act in a particular way in the course of your daily
   life or work?

>>Pray (5 minutes)
The discipline of listening

This exercise is probably best done using silent prayer, but if the
group wishes to pray out loud, agree that before beginning. The leader
speaks the words in italics.

Leader: *Be still and know that I am God . . .*
The leader then invites everyone to be quiet and allow the thoughts and
conversations of the session to settle.
Leader: *Send out your light and truth that they may lead us . . .*

Leader: *Rejoice in the Lord always . . .*
The leader invites everyone to recall any ways in the past (such as turning
outwards, anger, grief, grace, the negative way, prayer or other means)
through which we have sensed God's call in our lives. Give thanks to God
for this awareness of his presence with us.
Leader: *The angel of the Lord encamps around those who fear him, and
delivers them . . .*

Leader: *He will give you the desires of your heart . . .*
The leader invites everyone, in silent prayer, to name what they see as
God's calling for them to be or do in their present life. Name before God
the things we need to be faithful and fruitful for him in.
Leader: *Trust in the Lord and be doing good . . .*

Leader: *One thing is needful . . .*
The leader invites everyone to offer to God a specific step or action to
take in the coming days that would enable us to move forward in living
out of a sense of call from God.
Leader: *Trust in the Lord and he will bring it to pass . . .*

Pray together:

**Almighty God,
by whose grace alone we are accepted
and called to your service:
strengthen us by your Holy Spirit
and make us worthy of our calling;
through Jesus Christ your Son our Lord,
who is alive and reigns with you,
in the unity of the Holy Spirit,
one God, now and for ever. Amen.**
Collect for the Fifth Sunday before Lent, Common Worship, *p.*
387

>>Practise! (5 minutes)

Try one of the following. Be prepared to report back on your experience at the start of the next session.

Journal reflection:

Read the following quotation slowly, watching out for connections with your own experience.

I have mentioned that obedience is part of responding to God's call, and that's true, but it's not like a cut-and-dried military exercise. It's not as if we have to jump to attention when the divine command is boomed out on a loudspeaker. Part of the good news of Jesus Christ is being set free from rules, and not having to prove that we are good enough. We are not meant to live in slavish obedience to the old, written law, but in the freedom of God's Spirit. It is about having the impossible burden of getting life 'right' replaced with an invitation to follow the Lord of love.

Christina Rees, The Divine Embrace, *p. 102*

Take time to copy this passage into your journal. Write slowly and meditatively.

When you have finished, take a tea/coffee break.

Then return to your journal, take a clean page and, using bullet points, jot down the key aspects of the passage that have remained with you. Use these bullet points as a basis for prayer.

Talk with a friend/prayer partner about:
how God might be inviting you to participate in 'the movement of his love towards people,' (see Bosch quotation, p. 50).

Practise the spiritual discipline of listening
> let go of pressures, burdens, expectations and worries;
> meditate on the Scriptures;
> pay particular attention to conversations you have this week: note in your journal, any comments that strike you.

Keep a watch: when viewing TV, reading newspapers or
magazines, keep and ear/eye open for comments people make about their sense of call or life goals. Make a note in your journal and share with the group at the next session.

Start a conversation: with someone outside the membership
of the church and work at listening to both the words they are saying and the feeling they are communicating. Try using responses such as:
> 'am I right in thinking you are?'
> 'how does all that make you feel?'
Be prepared to share in the same way yourself. Expect to learn.

>>Aim

To explore what it means to live life out of a sense of call from God.

What you will need (make your own selection)

> Journal for all;
> DVD of the film *Billy Elliot*;
> Plasticine or play dough and other art materials.

>>Background

Leaders: for tips on making the most of the background material see p. 6.

We know more about David than almost any other biblical character. Considering his story can help us reflect on our experience of God's call. The aspects of God's call looked at in the course are well demonstrated in David's life. Looking at them helps us to locate where we are in our journey of faith. These aspects are:

> **Called by name:** God's choice of David was very personal. The prophet Samuel summoned all the other sons of Jesse, apparently more appropriate candidates for king, but God specifically wanted David. God chose the youngest, the one not considered important enough to be present. Human power and status do not score highly with God – 'not many of you were wise by human standards, not many were powerful, not many were of noble birth' (1 Corinthians 1.26). God's choice and call is sheer gift, coming out of God's grace not our worthiness, to be received by faith with thanksgiving. (See Dewar quotation on p. 61.)

> **Called from within:** though the call of God is a gift from outside us, it connects with and sparks into life his image deep within us. God identified in David 'a man after his own heart' (1 Samuel 13.14). What begins with the gift of God in choosing us, takes root in our character and choices. Despised

and alone for long hours with only sheep for company, David learned fast. He learned not only the skills to protect his life and his flock but, most importantly, the ability to trust God. Our call is rooted in the secret place of the heart, in the choices we make and the skills we develop (see O'Connor quotation on p. 62). God's call is first of all a call to keep ourselves in tune with his character.

> **Called out:** The story of Bathsheba, culminating in David's planning the death of her husband to cover his tracks, is evidence of his struggles with false paths to fulfilment. For us those urges and idols come easily to the surface, whether with sudden temptation or the slow erosion of faith and obedience. The really important thing when we fail is not that we have failed, but what we do with our failure (see Julian of Norwich quotation on p. 62). Out of David's honesty about his wrongdoing, God brought good, not least in the gift to us of his response as recorded in Psalm 51.

[3] Against you, you alone, have I sinned,
and done what is evil in your sight.

[6] You desire truth in the inward being;
therefore teach me wisdom in my secret heart.

[10] Create in me a clean heart, O God,
and put a new and right spirit in me.

> **Called up:** David, like us, did not initially discern the purpose of his calling. His first, public, step into obeying the call of God resulted in the defeat of Goliath. It was accomplished by a faith nurtured in secret and through skills honed over the years. In time he became the greatest king of Israel, one whom the prophets saw as an icon of the Messiah. His story was part of a much bigger story. For David, and for us, God's call enlists us in his loving purposes for all that is – far beyond our small, and often narrow, ambitions. (See the William Abraham quotation on p. 62.)

> **Called on:** David's life is the story of a remarkable journey
> from shepherd lad to sovereign king. There were many twists
> and turns, remarkable events and skills developed on the way.
> So, for us, there are many stages, challenges and new
> ventures in our following God. His call never ceases; and
> though we do not know what the future holds, we do know who
> holds it (see Rees quotation on p. 62).

Bible passage background: God says no to David (2 Samuel 7.1-17)

Here we find David in a moment of rest in his life, given him by God (v. 1), getting in touch with a long-held dream, which he shares with his trusted adviser, the prophet Nathan. (Hopefully this course has given us a similar opportunity to reflect and share our hopes and sense of call from God.)

Though he has come so far, from shepherd lad (v. 8) to one whose kingdom will last for ever (v. 13), there remain unfulfilled longings (v. 2). Notice that, although he is a powerful king, he goes to the prophet to discover the mind of God (v. 2).

On this occasion David receives a 'no' that surprises both the prophet and David (v. 5). Yet this 'no' is because of a bigger 'yes'. Great though David's plans are, God's purposes are greater. Discovering what God is calling us to do requires sharing our hopes and desires in prayer and (if possible) with a trusted friend. David is surprised by God's desire to outgive him (v. 11), opening his vision to a greater kingdom than he could ever have imagined (v. 13). This is a kingdom of which we, through the coming of Christ, have become inheritors (v. 16). We also share the same relationship with God and the same call to be caught up in his loving and generous purposes for this and future generations.

>>Welcome (5 minutes)

Welcome people back to the final session of the course. The aim is to consider God's call on our lives as we journey through life. We also look back over the course as a whole and draw out implications for our lives after the course has finished.

>>Pray (5–10 minutes)

A psalm of God's call to journey in faith (Psalm 23)

Read it, or download the text from **www.chpublishing.co.uk/lifecalling** and produce enough copies for everyone to say it together (alternate verses by men/women, two halves of the room or leader/group).

Pause for silent reflection and prayer.

Close by praying together the course prayer:

> **Eternal God,**
> **the light of the minds that know you,**
> **the joy of the hearts that love you,**
> **and strength of the wills that serve you:**
> **grant us so to know you**
> **that we may truly love you,**
> **and so to love you**
> **that we may truly serve you,**
> **whose service is perfect freedom;**
> **through Jesus Christ our Lord. Amen.**
>
> *after St Augustine of Hippo, AD 430*

>>Action replay (5 minutes)

Invite group members to talk about the practice they agreed to do last week.

Encourage people to share snippets from their journals if appropriate.

>>Time to share (5 minutes)

Use the following quotations to help you reflect on the
questions below.

The Father has put us into the world, not to walk through it with lowered
eyes, but to search for him through things, events, people. Everything
must reveal God to us.

Michel Quoist, quoted in Ruth Etchells, Just as I am, *p. 18*

To accept Christ is to accept a call to a constant and even cataclysmic
change in who you are and in how you think and respond to those around
you. To embrace Christ is to embrace inspection and change, to embrace
renewal and transformation both humbly and dauntlessly.

Fred Stoeker, quoted at www.pilgrimsmap.com/Quotes.html

Share together ways in which this has happened in your life, and how this
has happened during this course.

Have you seen this at work in the lives of others you know or have heard
or read about?

>>Encounter (20–25 minutes)

a. Input: whole-life calling (5 minutes)

Leader: using the background information on pp. 57–9, give a
brief introduction to the five aspects of calling explored in the course.

Something to think about . . .

On being called by God

'Knowing yourself to be loved by God'
is an ever deepening process
that may take a lifetime.

Francis Dewar, Live for a Change, *p. 4*

On being called from within

We ask to know the will of God
without guessing
that his will is written into our very beings.

Elizabeth O'Connor, in Francis Dewar's Invitations, *p. 17*

On being called out

The best prayer is to rest in the goodness of God,
knowing that that goodness can reach right down
to our lowest depths of need.

Julian of Norwich

On being called up

To be initiated into the rule of God
is to encounter a transcendent reality that has entered history
and to find oneself drawn up into
the ultimate purposes of God for history and creation.

William Abraham, The Logic of Evangelism, *p. 101*

On being called on

There has been no sense of arrival,
just the sense of knowing myself to be on the right path.
I have no idea where the path will continue to lead,
only the confidence in the One who is leading.

Christina Rees, The Divine Embrace, *p. 109*

---

b. Read about how God said no to David (5 minutes)
2 Samuel 7.1-17 (NRSV)

¹ Now when the king was settled in his house, and the Lord had given him rest from all his enemies around him, ² the king said to the prophet Nathan, 'See now, I am living in a house of cedar, but the ark of God stays in a tent.' ³ Nathan said to the king, 'Go, do all that you have in mind; for the Lord is with you.'

⁴ But that same night the word of the Lord came to Nathan: ⁵ Go and tell my servant David: Thus says the Lord: Are you the one to build me

a house to live in? [6] I have not lived in a house since the day I brought up the people of Israel from Egypt to this day, but I have been moving about in a tent and a tabernacle. [7] Wherever I have moved about among all the people of Israel, did I ever speak a word with any of the tribal leaders of Israel, whom I commanded to shepherd my people Israel, saying, 'Why have you not built me a house of cedar?' [8] Now therefore thus you shall say to my servant David: Thus says the Lord of hosts: I took you from the pasture, from following the sheep to be prince over my people Israel; [9] and I have been with you wherever you went, and have cut off all your enemies from before you; and I will make for you a great name, like the name of the great ones of the earth. [10] And I will appoint a place for my people Israel and will plant them, so that they may live in their own place, and be disturbed no more; and evildoers shall afflict them no more, as formerly, [11] from the time that I appointed judges over my people Israel; and I will give you rest from all your enemies. Moreover, the Lord declares to you that the Lord will make you a house. [12] When your days are fulfilled and you lie down with your ancestors, I will raise up your offspring after you, who shall come forth from your body, and I will establish his kingdom. [13] He shall build a house for my name, and I will establish the throne of his kingdom for ever. [14] I will be a father to him, and he shall be a son to me. When he commits iniquity, I will punish him with a rod such as mortals use, with blows inflicted by human beings. [15] But I will not take my steadfast love from him, as I took it from Saul, whom I put away from before you. [16] Your house and your kingdom shall be made sure for ever before me; your throne shall be established for ever. [17] In accordance with all these words and with all this vision, Nathan spoke to David.

c. Talk about it (15 minutes)

Consider together any of the following:

1. Why do you think God said 'no' to David?

2. Share any ways in which you have experienced a 'no' from God, and what has resulted from that.

3. What sort of journey did God's call take David on and what are the implications for our lives?

4. Who is, or can be, Nathan to us?

>>Do something (20 minutes)

1. Watch two clips from the film *Billy Elliot*. Introduce the first extract with the following:

Billy and his family are awaiting the result of his audition.

Watch the film from chapter 15 (01:26:56), when the toast pops up, to chapter 16 (01:03:53), when Billy says, 'I got in'.

In what ways does Billy's response reflect the fear that is often associated with pursuing God's calling?

Introduce the second extract with the following:

Billy, like us, has no idea where the pursuit of his calling will take him. This clip ties together his early promise and his later accomplishment.

Watch the film from chapter 17 (01:38:56), when we see the dancers backstage, to chapter 18 (01:43:43), when the final piece of music, 'I believe', plays out over the credits.

In what sense can we draw inspiration from the story of *Billy Elliot* as we consider the ongoing journey of living out our callings?

2. In groups, read the Methodist Covenant Prayer carefully. Each person is to select a phrase that particularly strikes them. Using plasticine, play dough (see web site for recipe) or other art materials, each person produces a visual picture to represent their phrase. Put all these pieces of artwork together and discuss what they say about your group response to this prayer of commitment.

I am no longer my own but yours.
Put me to what you will,
rank me with whom you will;
put me to doing, put me to suffering;

let me be employed for you or laid aside for you,
exalted for you or brought low for you.
Let me be full, let me be empty,
let me have all things, let me have nothing.
I freely and wholeheartedly yield all things
 to your pleasure and disposal.
And now, glorious and blessed God,
Father, Son and Holy Spirit,
you are mine and I am yours.
So be it.
And the covenant made on earth,
let it be ratified in heaven.
Amen.

>>Apply within (10 minutes)

Work together on any of the following questions, each person
choosing the question with which they want to work.

1. What are the issues raised for you by this session, and course,
   and what steps can you take to act on the insights gained?

2. In your journey of faith in response to the call of God, how
   would you describe where you are at present? For example:

   > at a junction having to choose which path to take;

   > involved in a steep climb;

   > where there is no clear path;

   > or how else would you describe your journey at present?

3. What do you see as your next steps in responding to God's
   call? What do you consider God might want you to bring into
   being in the months (and years?) ahead?

>>Pray (5 minutes)
The discipline of obedience

The vital step on the path of obedience is to surrender our lives, our plans and our priorities to God, and allow him to call us on into his greater purposes – just as David found.

Be still for two minutes and seek to discern what God is calling you on to in the light of this session and course. Prayerfully seek to discern how God's call enables you to complete the sentence 'In the coming days I see God calling me on to . . .' – not as moral pressure, but as life-giving invitation.

Then, as a group:

> > share those completed sentences (without discussion);

> > or pray (silently or aloud) for one another;

> > or proceed straight to . . .

Conclude by praying together (either, or both):

> > **The Methodist Covenant Prayer** (turn back to p. 64)

> > The **course prayer** (turn back to p. 60).

>>Practise! (5 minutes)

Develop a Personal Action Plan for discerning your vocation in the whole of life. Spend such time as is available sharing in small groups your response to any of the following steps where you have a clear answer at present. Then agree how you might (as a whole group or in your small group) continue to develop such a plan in the coming weeks and months. It may be good to seek out someone (not necessarily a member of the group) with whom you could talk this over in the months ahead.

Such a plan might include taking the following steps:

1. Put it in your own words

On paper and/or in conversation with a prayer partner, express your sense of call – such as it is – right now. It is a vital starting point. Expect it to grow.

2. Narrow the search area

You may find it helpful to separate out home life and closest relationships, church life, work, hobbies, wider society and seek to discern God's call in any one of these. However, be open to some overarching sense of call on your life.

3. Listen to yourself

Make a note of your longings, dreams, hopes, desires and see if there is any emerging focus or direction in this. What 'makes you tick'?

4. Listen to others

Talk with others about their sense of call and about yours. We can learn much from seeing how a sense of call shapes the lives of others and by the discipline of putting into words what we sense is our call.

5. Listen to God

This will really be enhanced by keeping a journal and making a note of any insights from the following sources:

> acts of worship;

> meditating on the Scriptures;

> prayer (and what you feel led to pray about);

> conversations (a thought or response may stay with you);

> intuitions: sometimes things leap out of the blue and speak to us or prompt us to take action.

Expect and be open to God the Spirit in all the above. It is the Spirit who breathes life into all our longings (Romans 8.26-27).

See Discovering God's Call in the Appendix (or web site) for further guidance on these elements.

>>Ways in which we can discover God's call

> Worship

Giving attention to God and taking delight in who he is and his nature enables us to get a right perspective on life and our part in God's purposes of love. This involves the giving of ourselves to God in corporate worship and personal devotions.

> Scripture

The Scriptures have been the key means of guidance to many saints down the centuries. This is most likely to happen if we read them slowly, meditate upon them and use them to inspire our prayer to God about our own lives.

> Intercession

In prayer we express God's compassion for others, make ourselves available for his purposes in and through us and bring our own plans before God for him to bless, direct and challenge.

> Conversation

It is often the casual remark of another person that sparks some insight in us that can become a formative influence on the direction our lives take. We need to be open to God speaking to us in our ordinary daily conversations.

> Intuition

Sometimes insights, possibilities, opportunities and 'answers' come, seemingly out of the blue. They are sometimes like seeing a kingfisher – a rare flash of colour, gone in a moment. If we are alive to God in the whole of our living we can catch these insights and see in them the call of God on our lives.

> Life

As someone has said, 'every experience is a kind of annunciation' and God can speak to us through nature, through our senses, our reading, things we see and hear and experiences that happen to us. Our calling is to be alive to God in the whole of life and to 'expect the unexpected'.

> The Holy Spirit

Sometimes we may sense some insight or 'burden' as coming directly by inspiration of the Spirit. The more usual way in which we experience the guidance of the Spirit of God is in and through all the previous six ways.

Mrs Fidget very often said that she lived for her family. And it was not untrue. Everyone in the neighbourhood knew it. 'She lives for her family,' they said: 'what a wife and mother!' She did all the washing; true, she did it badly and they could have afforded to send it but to a laundry, and they frequently begged her not to do it. But she did. There was always a hot lunch for anyone who was at home and always a hot meal at night (even in midsummer). They implored her not to provide this. They protested almost with tears in their eyes (and with truth) that they liked cold meals. It made no difference. She was living for her family. She always sat up to 'welcome' you if you were out late at night; two or three in the morning, it made no odds; you would always find the frail, pale, weary face awaiting you, like a silent accusation. Which meant, of course, that you couldn't with any decency go out very often. She was always making things too; being in her own estimation (I'm no judge myself) an excellent amateur dressmaker and a great knitter. And, of course, unless you were a heartless brute, you had to wear the things. (The vicar tells me that, since her death, the contributions of that family alone to 'sales of work' outweigh those of all his other parishioners put together.) . . . Mrs Fidget, as she so often said, would 'work her fingers to the bone' for her family. They couldn't stop her. Nor could they – being decent people – quite sit still and watch her do it. They had to help. Indeed they were always having to help. That is, they did things for her to help her to do things for them, which they didn't want done. As for the dear dog, it was to her, she said, 'just like one of the children'. It was in fact as like one of them as she could make it. But since it had no scruples it got on rather better than they, and though vetted, dieted and guarded within an inch of its life, contrived sometimes to reach the dustbin or the dog next door.

The vicar says Mrs Fidget is now at rest. Let us hope she is. What's quite certain is that her family are.

from C. S. Lewis, *The Four Loves*

>> Bibliography

William Abraham, *The Logic of Evangelism*, Wm B. Eerdmans Publishing Company, 1989.

Archbishops' Council, *Common Worship: Services and Prayers for the Church of England*, Church House Publishing, 2000.

Michael Baughen, *Hymns for Today's Church* (revised edn), Hodder & Stoughton Religious, 1987.

David Bosch, *Transforming Mission*, Orbis, 1991.

Brother Lawrence, *Practising the Presence of God, and the Spiritual Maxims*, Cosimo Inc., 2006.

Common Praise, Canterbury Press, 2000.

S. Cottrell, S. Croft, J. Finney, F. Lawson and R. Warren, *Emmaus: Leading an Emmaus Group*, Church House Publishing, 1998, second edition 2004.

Francis Dewar, *Invitations*, SPCK, 1996.

Francis Dewar, *Live for a Change*, Darton, Longman & Todd, 1988.

David Ford, *The Shape of Living*, HarperCollins, 1997.

Gerard Hughes, *God of Surprises*, Darton, Longman & Todd, 1985.

C. S. Lewis, *The Four Loves*, Fount, 1998.

Gerard May, *Addiction and Grace*, HarperCollins, 1991.

Janet Morley, *All Desires Known*, SPCK, 1992.

Leanne Payne, *The Healing Presence*, Baker Publishing, 1995.

Longman Dictionary of Contemporary English, Longman, 1987.

Ruth Etchells, *Just as I am*, SPCK, 1995.

Timothy Radcliffe, *What is the Point of Being a Christian?*, Burns & Oates, 2005.

Christina Rees, *The Divine Embrace*, Darton, Longman & Todd, 2006.

George Bernard Shaw, *Man and Superman*, Constable & Co. Ltd, 1929, pp. xxxi–xxxii.

Shorter Oxford Dictionary, Oxford University Press, 1933.

Rick Warren, *The Purpose Driven Life*, Zondervan, 2002.

Dallas Willard, *In Search of Guidance*, Zondervan, 1993.

E is for discipleship

Running Alpha, Christianity Explored or another Christian basics course and struggling to know what to do next? Looking for small group material that's not mind-bogglingly academic or mind-numbingly shallow? Help is at hand.

The 'Emmaus – the Way of Faith' discipleship material offers a library of stand-alone modules that are designed to help Christians develop and grow. Each module is split into four or five sessions which provide material for Bible study, discussion, group exercises, meditations, practical application and prayers. There's plenty of background material for leaders and a series of downloadable handouts for each member of the study group.

Emmaus encourages a journey of faith that is life-changing, enduring and that has a positive impact on the community of believers, as well as the individual.

Curious? Call 020 7898 1451 today and request a FREE Introduction to Emmaus Pack, email emmaus@c-of-e.org.uk or visit **www.e-mmaus.org.uk** for full details.

Emmaus – the first word in discipleship